Voyager Passport E

Fluency

1

ISBN 978-1-4168-0569-4

Table of Contents

Fluency Practice

 Read the story to each other.

 Read the story on your own.

 Read the story to your partner again. Try to read the story even better.

 Questions? Ask your partner two questions about the story. Tell each other about the story you just read.

Timed Reading

1. When you do a timed reading with your partner, make sure that you have practiced your story and know all the words.

2. When you are ready, tell your partner to start the timer.

3. Read carefully, and your partner will stop you at 1 minute. When you stop, mark your place.

4. Count the total number of words you read.

5. In the back of your Student Book, write the number of words you read and color in the squares on your Fluency Chart.

6. Now switch with your partner.

Northern Lights

It looks like lights dancing in the sky or an amazing fireworks display. The night sky lights up in red, green, blue, and violet streaks of light. What is this crazy light show? It's called the Northern Lights. The Northern Lights can be seen from countries in the far north. They appear mostly in the sky in the Arctic region.

In Finland, a story says that an Arctic fox started fires with its tail. They call the lights "fox fires." (80)

The real story is that the sun causes the Northern Lights. The sun gives off energy bits. These bits form a cloud, which moves like a stream. This cloud is called the solar wind. The solar wind flows to Earth and bumps into gases around Earth. This causes a glow. That beautiful glow is the Northern Lights.

A Roar in the Woods

Quinn stepped out of his cousin's van and looked around. He'd never been out of the city. All the hikers put on their backpacks and headed down the trail. ㉙

The first thing Quinn noticed was the quiet. Then, he listened more closely. There were the sounds of crunching sticks and leaves under hiking boots, birds chirping high in the trees, and his lunch rustling in his backpack. ㉗

Slowly, the trail turned and got steeper. Quinn heard a new, faint sound. The trail turned again, and suddenly the faint sound became a roar. Was there a subway, a train, or a big truck out here in the woods? ⑩⑦

Quinn looked and listened more closely. At the top of the hill, Quinn and his cousin stopped. The roar was so loud they had to shout over the sound. All that noise came from water. It flowed over rocks and became white and foamy. ⑮①

Quinn discovered the cause of the roar. It was the roar of a waterfall.

Team Colors

Madison's favorite coach was Ms. Acosta. Madison wanted to give Ms. Acosta a gift, but she didn't have any money. Madison sat with her head in her hands. She twirled her necklace on her finger. Then, she had an idea.

Madison stirred salt, flour, and water. She cooked the mixture until it was thick. Then, she rolled the dough into little balls. She used a toothpick to make a hole through the middle of each ball to make beads. Then, she baked the beads in the oven. ⑧⑦

Madison spread newspapers outside. She waited for the beads to cool. She painted half the beads green and half the beads gold. Madison placed a gold bead on a string. Then, she added a green bead. She filled the string with gold and green beads. Finally, she tied the string in a knot. Madison had made a necklace for Ms. Acosta in the team colors of green and gold.

Dad's Concert in the Park

"Wait for me!" yelled Emma. Her younger brother Michael ran toward a big oak tree.

"How about right here?" asked Michael. Emma nodded. Their mother spread out a big blanket on the ground. People began to fill the city park for the afternoon concert.

"I hope Dad can see us," said Michael. "The park is starting to get crowded."

"Don't worry," said Emma. "Remember what Dad told us this morning. The concert won't start until he knows we are here." ⑧⓪

The musicians took their seats. The conductor looked out at the crowd of people. "There's Dad," yelled Michael. "Hello, Dad! Look over here!" Michael tried to shout over the noisy crowd. "I don't think he can hear me," Michael said sadly.

Just then, the conductor waved his arms in the air. The musicians began to play. "See, Michael? Dad started the concert for us," said Emma. "He must have heard you after all." Michael smiled and gave Emma a big hug. It sure was fun to watch Dad conduct a concert in the park.

Seeing Stars

"It's movie time!" shouted Derek. "Race you to the van!" He picked up his goggles and sprinted past Anna. ⑲

Anna had no idea what Derek was talking about. She knew they were going to Sunset Pool at Midview City Park. Anna climbed into the van and sat next to Derek. ㊿

"Ready for the movie?" asked Dad. ㊶

"What are you talking about?" Anna asked. "I thought we were going swimming." ㉖⑨

"Don't you remember?" asked Derek. "It's Flick and Float Night at the pool. Everyone watches a movie and floats on the water." ㉑①

Anna looked up at the night sky and chuckled. "Gee, I can't wait to tell my friends that I saw stars at the movies!"

Let's Get Moving

"Closed for repairs," said Quincy, staring at the sign by the train. "I can't believe it. Old Red's been here forever."

"I know," said Kayla. "I rode on Old Red for the first time when I was a baby." Kayla followed Quincy up the path to the visitor's center. They found out that the train needed a new engine, but the park was low on funds. ⑯

"I've got an idea," said Quincy. Soon Kayla and Quincy finished their signs at the city art center. Then, they found a big jar and wrote "Save Old Red" across the front.

"Let's stand by Old Red to collect money," said Kayla.

"Good idea," said Quincy. "We'd better get moving so Old Red can too!"

Wild Things in the Park

Are you a nature lover? Spring and summer are perfect seasons to sign up for a city park nature walk. Pack up a hand lens and a camera. You might want to take along a notebook too. (37)

The nature tour leader speaks to your group. “Don’t chase the wild things. Let them come to you.” You jot down what she says along with several new facts. (66)

As you walk along the dirt path that winds through the park, the leader points out many of the park’s occupants. Look! It’s a robin—the first sign of spring. You notice an endangered falcon resting in the treetops, and you snap a picture. Bees buzz around wildflowers in full bloom. A lizard basks on a large rock. (124)

There are all sorts of interesting plants, but don’t touch that one! It has three leaves. Suddenly you remember something you wrote down earlier. “Leaves of three, let them be.” Oh no, poison ivy! That’s one wild thing you don’t want to encounter. (167)

A Living Part of History

Have you ever been to Philadelphia? It has one of the largest city parks in the world. It's a chain of parks called Fairmount Park. The park is just minutes away from any part of the city.

Fairmount Park is home to more than 1 million trees. People can walk, skate, or ride their bikes along miles of paths. (59)

Fairmount Park is a living part of history too. Just look around. You can stop at one of its 200 statues. Many nearby buildings are more than 100 years old.

What else can you find? You can see the oldest zoo in our country. Fairmount Park is a fun place to learn about our past!

Living in the Dark Zone

There are some creatures most people have never seen. These creatures never see you either. They live in the dark zone. The dark zone isn't a place in outer space. It's the area deep within a cave.

This cool, dark zone is home to all sorts of animals. Sunlight never reaches the dark zone. Many of these animals cannot see, such as the blind crayfish. Yet this is not a problem. Animals that live here must use other senses to stay alive. (82)

Some dark zone animals have no eyes. The Texas Blind Salamander is one example. The Texas Blind Salamander has two small black dots under its skin where eyes would be found. It hunts in cave water for tiny snails and shrimp.

How can it find food if it can't see? It hunts for food in a special way. A snail or shrimp makes small waves when it moves in the water. The salamander can feel where the waves come from. Then, it knows that dinner is close by. Watch out, snail!

Prairie Dog Town

Prairie dogs are not what they seem to be. Sure, they live on the prairie, but they are not dogs at all! A prairie dog is really a type of ground squirrel. Prairie dogs live in the western part of the United States and Mexico.

Prairie dogs prefer to live in large groups. These groups are made up of burrows, called towns. Prairie dogs search for food in the day and return to their burrows to sleep at night.⑦⑨ They mostly eat grass, seeds, leaves, flowers, and fruit. Sometimes prairie dogs will eat an occasional insect or two.

Many prairie animals like to hunt prairie dogs. What does a prairie dog do when a wolf, fox, or bobcat sneaks up on it ready to pounce? Zip! The prairie dog scrambles into its burrow. Whew! That was a close one!

Danger, Rattlesnakes!

Nick always played tricks on Tran. "I think it's time I teach Nick a lesson," said Tran. He gathered his things and sat down at the table. "A little bit of his own medicine should do the trick," said Tran. Then, he began to work.

First, Tran straightened a large paper clip. Next, he bent it into a wide U. Then, he pulled the rubber band through two holes in a button. He stretched the rubber band around both ends of the paper clip.⑧④ Then, Tran wrote across the front of an envelope in big bold letters. It read: *Danger, Rattlesnakes!* He carefully flipped the button over dozens of times. Now the rubber band was twisted very tightly. Tran placed the whole thing inside the envelope. Then, he hid behind the sofa and waited for Nick.

Nick walked into the room and read the words aloud. "Danger, Rattlesnakes!" Nick said. He peeked inside the envelope and the button let loose. It rattled against the paper clip. "Aaahhhh!" yelled Nick. That sure was a lesson he'd never forget!

Father Goose

Just about everyone has heard the name Mother Goose. But, not many people know about a real man called Father Goose. "Father Goose" is the nickname of Bill Lishman. In 1994, Bill led 18 Canada geese south for the winter.

Bill Lishman was a metal sculptor and an inventor. He and his family lived in Canada. Bill loved animals and flying. One day, he and his family saw a film called *Skyward*. It showed geese that followed a boat. "I wonder if geese would follow a plane?" he asked himself. He asked an animal trainer for help. ⓐ⁷

Bill knew that some birds were in danger of losing their habitat. So, Bill decided to help them. He wanted to try first with Canada geese. The geese were not in danger though. If Bill could teach the geese, he knew he'd be able to help birds that were at risk.

Bill kept many geese eggs on his farm. He watched them every day and waited for them to hatch. When geese hatch, they follow the first thing they see. This is called imprinting. Bill wanted the geese to imprint on him. Then, they would follow and learn from him, as if he were their parent.

The big day arrived! The geese hatched from their eggs. Bill was right there watching. He put the baby birds under heat lamps to stay warm. When they were strong enough, Bill taught them how to chase after him. ⓐ⁰³

One day, Bill climbed into his small ultralight plane and drove around. The geese chased after Bill and his plane. A few days later, Bill flew the plane in the air. When he looked behind him, he saw an incredible sight. The geese were flying after him!

Fly Away Home

Bill could hardly believe it! His plan had worked. The geese followed behind him as he flew the ultralight. But, were the geese up for their big task? Could Bill teach them to fly south for the winter? These geese did not know how. They did not grow up in the wild. Winters in Canada were harsh and cold. If the geese did not fly south, they could die.(69)

Each day, Bill flew the plane, and the geese flew behind him. Bill made sure that each trip was longer than the one before it. He wanted the geese to build up their strength to fly south in the fall. He knew their migration to Virginia would be a long one. Would they be able to make it?

On a crisp, autumn day in 1994, Bill knew he'd find out. Bill "Father Goose" Lishman and 18 Canada geese began their flight from Canada to Virginia. Bill hoped the geese would make it to their warm habitat.(165)

Not only did the geese arrive safely, they remembered their migration path. By the following spring, the geese had returned to Canada. Bill's plan was a success! Now he could begin his work with birds that were in danger of losing their habitats. He could teach them to migrate to new places. Then, they would be safe.

Since then, Bill and others have formed Operation Migration. Bill has led other types of birds to safe places. Now these birds are growing in number.(248)

You may think that Bill's work seems like something that happens in a movie. You are right. In 1996, a movie was made about Bill and his geese. It was called *Fly Away Home*. A movie always comes to an end though. Luckily, Bill's work with birds does not end. Thanks to Father Goose, birds in danger now have a chance to fly away home!

Flying Seeds

Have you ever picked a dandelion, blown its seeds, and made a wish? If you have, then you have helped nature!

Adult plants make seeds. These seeds need to get away from the adult plants because the big plants take all of the sunlight and water that the little seeds need. Some seeds can travel far away from the big plants.

A poppy has seeds in a pouch.⑱ When the wind blows, the pouch opens. The seeds fly into the air.

Dandelion seeds have a fluffy parachute on top. The parachute traps the wind. The seeds can stay in the air for a long time.

Maple seeds look like wings. When the wind blows, the seeds spin around and around before they fall to the ground. They look like little helicopters.

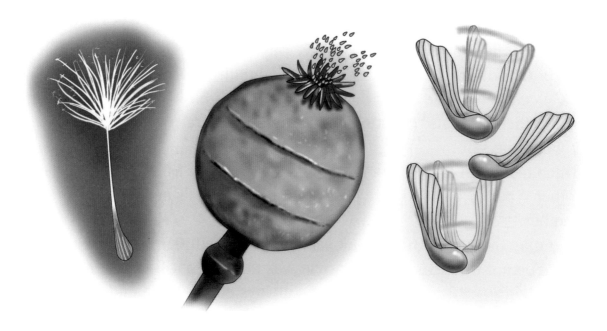

Helicopters

Unlike an airplane, a helicopter has its blades on top. The blades are called a rotor. When the rotor turns fast, the helicopter takes off. ㉕

Helicopters have different numbers of blades. A small helicopter has a two-blade rotor. Larger helicopters can carry more people. These helicopters might have a four-blade rotor. ㊳

To make a helicopter move, the pilot tilts the rotor. By moving the rotor, the pilot can make the helicopter move right and left or forward and backward. A helicopter does not need a runway. Instead, it can rise straight up. It can even stop in the air like a hummingbird. ⑭

Helicopters have many uses. You might see one in a large city. Helicopters watch the traffic on the highways. They also can carry things, like heavy trucks, from place to place where there are no roads. Watch the sky for a helicopter. Why is it being used?

Catcher Can Climb

As Saul and Catcher walked through the park, Catcher bounced up and down excitedly. Every Saturday, Saul took her to the park for a game of Frisbee.

Saul put down the bag he was carrying. He reached in and pulled out a bright pink Frisbee. Catcher barked and wagged her tail.

"Okay, girl," Saul said. "Are you ready?" Catcher barked her reply.

Saul flicked his wrist and sent the Frisbee sailing. Catcher jumped up and back, up and back, her eyes never leaving the pink Frisbee in the air. Ⓐ⁹

The Frisbee kept sailing. It landed in a tree! Catcher barked and looked at Saul. Saul stared up at the Frisbee, wondering what to do. Just then Catcher jumped to a low branch of the tree. She stood up on her back legs and grabbed the Frisbee with her teeth.

"Wow!" said Saul. "Maybe I need to call you Climber!"

Thanking Mrs. Williams

Elise opened the book that Mrs. Williams, the librarian, had helped her find. She wanted to win the class paper airplane contest. She looked through the pages. Some of the directions looked hard. Then she found it—the perfect paper airplane.

She found the two things she needed—paper and paper clips. She read the directions, looked at the pictures, and began folding. After 10 tries, Elise finished folding the airplane. She added the paper clips to the nose. Finally, she bent the back of the wings up, just a bit.

Now it was time for a test flight. Elise got Dad and took the airplane into the backyard.

"Ready? Go!" yelled Dad. (113)

Elise threw the airplane with all her might. It flew right past Dad! Elise jumped up and down with excitement. She took a yardstick and measured how far the plane had flown.

The next day, Elise took her airplane to school. There were all kinds of designs. Elise began to worry. "How far will their planes fly?" she wondered.

Mr. Boyd asked all the students to stand in a line with their airplanes. "Ready? Go!" he yelled. Everyone threw their planes as hard as they could.

After the planes landed, each of the students measured how far his or her plane had flown. Elise was the winner! Her plane had flown 25 feet! Mr. Boyd gave her an award. As she took it, she said, "Thank you, Mrs. Williams!"

Go Fly a Kite

What flew before the airplane or the hot air balloon? The answer is a kite! Over the years, kites have been flown for many reasons.

More than 2,000 years ago, an army in China had a problem. They wanted to attack people inside a castle. The army did not have many men. They built a kite. They flew the kite over the castle walls and over the middle of the castle. The men marked the kite string to know how far it was to the middle. Then the men dug a tunnel. They used the kite string to know how far to dig. The men came out of the tunnel in the middle of the castle. They surprised the people and won the fight.(124)

In 1822, people used horses to pull carts. A man used two large kites to pull a cart full of people. The kites pulled the cart faster than the horses could. But it had to be windy for the "flying car" to work.

People have even flown in kites. About 300 years ago, a man flew to the top of a castle in a kite. He stole some gold from the roof! He was caught when he bragged about what he had done. During times of war, people have flown in kites to spy on their enemies.

Today kites are used for fun. They also are used in sports. In 1999, a team used the power of a kite to pull a sled to the North Pole!

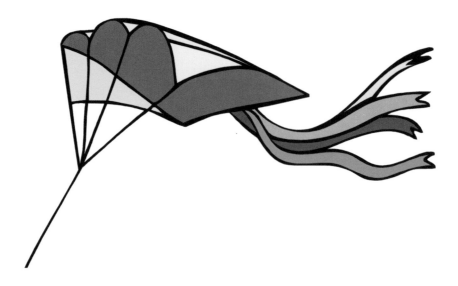

Aiko's Star Search

"It's not there!" Aiko exclaimed as she threw a book on the table.

"What's not there?" asked her older brother Taro.

"Leo the Lion," Aiko said with a sigh. "This book says you can look up at the night sky and connect the stars in your mind to find pictures of people and animals."

"Yes," said Taro. ⑤⑦

"Look at this one," Aiko said, pointing to a picture in the book. It was a group of stars that formed the outline of a lion. "This is Leo the Lion. I can't find these stars anywhere in the sky." ⑨⑦

"That's because it is December," Taro said calmly. "You can't see Leo this time of year. Come with me."

Taro took Aiko's hand and led her onto the lawn. "Look there," he said. "You can see Taurus the Bull."

"Where?" asked Aiko excitedly.

"Right there," said Taro pointing to the sky. "You can see its horns there and its feet there."

"I see it! I see it!" said Aiko. "Show me another one!" she said with a smile.

A Trip to the Mountains

"Pile into the car, everyone," said Dad. "We need to get going."

"Where are you taking us?" asked Brynne. "It's practically dark outside."

"Exactly," answered Dad. "We're headed for the mountains. You'll be amazed at what you see."

Brynne wrinkled her brows together. She looked at the setting sun, somewhat puzzled.

What could Dad possibly be thinking? Soon it would be pitch dark. They'd barely be able to see their own hands, much less something fascinating in the woods.

As Dad drove, Brynne wondered what he wanted to show them. Maybe they were going on a midnight opossum hunt. No, that didn't seem like something Dad would do.(108)

Perhaps he was taking them owl watching. No, there must be another reason. Just then, Dad drove the car up a winding road. Brynne spotted a large sign. It read "Hanson Observatory."

Brynne smiled. Of course! Now things were beginning to make sense. Observatories were always high up in the mountains. The view of the sky was so much clearer there.

Dad parked the car. Then he opened the door. "Everybody out," he said. "The sky is waiting for us."

Brynne jumped out of the car. Then she ran toward the building. "Let the star gazing begin!" she said happily.

Word List

placed	watch
double	can't
spread	saw
remember	ready
started	sign
sure	enough